LIGHTHOUSES OF MAINE AND NEW HAMPSHIRE

A PICTORIAL TOUR OF THE LIGHTHOUSES OF MAINE AND NEW HAMPSHIRE

ALL LIGHTHOUSES PAST AND PRESENT • HISTORICAL INFORMATION AND DIRECTIONS INCLUDED

BY KATHLEEN E. FINNEGAN AND TIMOTHY E. HARRISON

Front Cover: West Quoddy Head

Text, photography, and layout design by Timothy Harrison and Kathleen Finnegan.
Inside cover layout by Carol Cloutier, Brookside Studio, P.O. Box 1882, Wolfeboro, NH 03894
Color separation by Colortronix Corporation, 8025 S. Willow Street, Manchester, NH 03103
Printing by Quantum Printing Corporation, 32 Moulton Street, Laconia, NH 03246

Printed in the United States of America

Nothing can symbolize the maritime history of our country more than the lighthouse and the keepers who served them. Although the keepers and their families have gone into the pages of our history books, the lighthouse remains to remind us of our history and heritage to the sea.

This publication is dedicated to the memory of the keepers and their families, people who lived dangerous lives and served in isolation, in the protection of all vessels and crews regardless of origin. The history books are full of accounts of keepers risking their own lives with fantastic feats of heroism in the saving of lives. Their families often played as much a part, and sometimes more, in keeping the lights burning.

During our research for this publication, we found incomplete and conflicting dates of construction, destruction, heights, candlepower, etc., but one thing was never in dispute, and that was the many sacrifices and deeds of bravery of the keepers.

You will find in the pages, pictures of every lighthouse in Maine and New Hampshire. We have included their location, some brief information on the lighthouse, general information on the surrounding area, and in some cases a famous event that took place in the vicinity.

We sincerely hope that you will have the time to visit as many lighthouses as possible and perhaps you too, will take an interest in the significant role the lighthouse has played in the growth of America.

Each time you visit a lighthouse, take time to reflect and let your mind drift back in time and imagine what life was like a hundred years ago at this lighthouse. If you do, you will understand why we have dedicated this publication to the lighthouse keeper and their families.

Through the pages of this publication, it is our dream that you too may become a lighthouse enthusiast and by joining any one of the various lighthouse organizations, you will help in the preservation of a little slice of our American History.

MAINE

Nickname: Pine Tree State

2,500 lakes and ponds and 5,000 rivers and streams

Length of the coastline is 3,500 miles

2,000 coastal islands of which 700 are barren rocks

Became a state March 15, 1820, to be the 23rd state

Easternmost state of the United States

Eastport Maine is the easternmost city of the nation

Lubec Maine is the easternmost town of the mainland

Known as VACATIONLAND with an estimated 14 million visitors every year

Largest industries are: wood processing, fishing, agriculture, and tourism

Potatoes rank 3rd in acreage and 4th in production nationally

America's largest blueberry growing state raising 90% of the low-bush blueberries in North America

State fish: Salmo Salar Sebago, known more commonly as the landlocked salmon

State bird: Chickadee

State tree: White Pine

Maine lobster are flown to restaurants and stores all over the world

Has over 436,000 acres of state and national parks

Kittery is the oldest town in Maine, settled in 1624 and incorporated in 1647

Kittery Shipyard launched the U.S.S. Ranger in May 1777, which was the first vessel to fly the Stars & Stripes, and was commanded by John Paul Jones

As we travelled along the coast of Maine, we found that one of the best guides, was *The Illustrated Map of the Maine Coast.* It is available at most giftshops, gas stations and stores; however if you are unable to find it, you may order it from the DeLorme Mapping Company, P.O. Box 298 Freeport, Maine 04032, (207)865-4171.

MAINE NOTABLES

Joshua Chamberlain 1828-1914	Commander of 20th Maine Infantry in the Civil War and was present at Lee's surrender Governor 1867-1871
William Pitt Fessenden 1806-1869	U.S. House of Representatives 1840-1842 U.S. Senator 1854-1869 Cast the crucial NOT GUILTY vote at the impeachment trial of President Andrew Johnson
Hannibal Hamlin 1809-1891	U.S. House of Representatives 1843-1847 U.S. Senator 1847-1857 and 1869-1881 One of the original founders of the Republican Party First Republican Governer of Maine in 1857 Vice President under Abraham Lincoln 1861-1865
Winlow Homer 1836-1891	Famous artist who depicted Maine in his many nautical and seascape paintings
Henry Knox 1750-1806	Revolutionary War General and was the first U.S. SECRETARY OF WAR under President George Washington He built the mansion 'MONTPELLIER" which is located on the eastern bank of the Georges River at Thomaston, Maine
Henry Wadsworth Longfellow 1807-1882	Professor and world famous poet, who immortalized the Famous Midnight Ride of Paul Revere
Margaret Chase Smith 1897-	first female U.S. Senator U.S. Senator 1949-1972
Guy P. Gannett 1881-1954	Influential newspaperman and publisher Founder of Guy Gannett Broadcasting Services

Because of the large coastal trading industry, the dangerous coast of Maine with its rocky shore, reefs, ledges, and islands was the first land sighted by many vessels arriving from Europe. Since the rugged coast of Maine supported a large trading industry with its marine traffic, many of the earliest lighthouses in the nation were built along coastal Maine and New Hampshire.

For the protection of the ships, some lighthouses were built on rocky ledges or reefs totally exposed to the sea and for their time, were great engineering feats. Not only was a tremendous amount of skill involved, there was also great danger to the crews that constructed many of these lighthouses.

Among the Lighthouses of Maine and New Hampshire, you will be able to see many different styles, shapes, and sizes. Some are located in beautiful surroundings, while others stand alone on guard at some desolate island or dangerous reef.

The most fully equipped station consisted of the lighttower, fog signal building, keepers dwellings, oil house, boat house, and a landing wharf. At some stations it was necessary to make the tower and dwelling in the same structure.

You will find the people in all the coastal communities warm and friendly; however, while visiting these lighthouses please be sure to remember that many of the original keepers quarters are now private residences. Many of the areas around and near some lighthouses are private property; please remember to honor their privacy and show respect for their property.

ST. CROIX

Built in 1857, on beautiful Dochet Island at the entrance to the St. Croix River, St. Croix Lighthouse was the first light in the first lighthouse district Located at the official border of the United States and Canada, this lightstation was rebuilt in 1901 and automated in 1957.

Having been abandoned and without caretaker, the lighthouse fell in disrepair and became a hangout for young people. One chilly, windy night juveniles on the run from the police, took refuge in the old keeper's house. To keep warm they built a fire, which soon got out of control. Fueled by high winds the fire soon swept the island destroying the keeper's house and all the other buildings. This historic lighthouse, at the international border, is now gone forever.

Photograph above is courtesy of the National Archives, previous page courtesy of U.S Coast Guard.

WHITLOCKS MILL

Located on the south bank of the St. Croix River, near Calais, Maine, this active light was built in 1910 to replace the orignal light of 1892. The keepers quarters is now a private residence. Calais has the unique distinction of being halfway between the North Pole and the Equator on the 45th parallel.

The light can be easily photographed from the picnic area on US 1 just south of Calais.

LUBEC CHANNEL

This light was built in the west side of Lubec Channel in 1890. It is still active and has a green flashing light.

To reach the light take Route 189 from US 1 to Lubec, Maine, to the road marked Quoddy State Park.

MULHOLLAND

This inactive light, built in 1885, is on the east side of the channel on Campobello Island in Canada on Mulholland Point. From Rt 189 take the international bridge into Canada, just past the customs station will be an unmarked gravel road on the left which leads directly to the lighthouse. Do not stop on the International Bridge, you must stop and check in at the customs station first. There are picnic tables on the grounds but there are no washroom facilities available.

From this location you can also see and photograph Lubec Channel Light.

EAST QUODDY HEAD

This light, maintained by the Canadian Coast Guard, is located on the northern end of Campobello Island, Canada.

The fixed red light is to warn of the headlands jagged rocks. As a daymarker, the large red cross is to make it easier to see against a snowy background.

To reach this light proceed two miles past the customs station and turn right at the unmarked intersection. Follow this road about 15 miles, the last three being unpaved. The road dead ends at a small parking area. Follow the trail to a series of iron/rail stairways up and down the islands. When the tide is low, you can get very close to the light. Be very careful of the changing tides, since the water level changes five feet per hour and it is possible to get stranded on the island for eight hours.

While in the area, be sure to visit Franklin Roosevelt's summer home and Roosevelt Park. The International park is maintained by the Canadian and US Governments. It is well worth the time.

WEST QUODDY HEAD

The eastern-most point in the continental United States

This active light, which marks the southwest entrance to Quoddy Channel, was built in 1858. The original tower was built under the orders of Thomas Jefferson in 1807. The white flashing light is visible for 18 miles.

The light can be reached by taking route 189 to the road marked Quoddy State Park.

This state park is open daily, free to the public from May 30 to Labor Day and on weekends until November 1. Be sure to spend some time walking the nature trails along the high cliffs, which have railings separating the trail from the forty foot drop to the raging surf below.

The views from these trails are some of the most spectacular along the Atlantic Coast.

LITTLE RIVER

The Little River Light was built in 1847 and then rebuilt in 1975. The light can only be seen by air or by boat.

It is located on an off shore island at the mouth of the Little River in Cutler, Maine.

MACHIAS SEAL ISLAND

This light is maintained by the Canadian Government, although it is contained in Maine waters, twelve miles off the coast of Cutler, Maine.

The lighthouse, with its white flashing light can only be seen by air or by boat.

The island is the home of a large puffin colony, which is strickly protected by the Canadian Wildlife Service.

LIBBY ISLAND

Known for many years as Machias Light

Built in 1817 and refurbished in 1822, this light marks the southern entrance to Machias Bay, and can only be photographed by sea or air.

This area which is often draped in heavy fog, has been the spot of many famous shipwrecks: Ella G. Ellis, Caladonia, and the Sarah. The ballad *Loss of the Sarah* describes that wreck.

This is the eastern most lighthouse of the United States.

MOOSE PEAK

This light is located south of Jonesport on the east side of Mistake Island, 72 feet above the sea.

The tower was built in 1827 and has a 1.1 million candlepower flashing white light that can be seen for 26 miles.

AVERY ROCK

Built in 1875 on the southern end of Avery Rock, this light which marked the entrance to Machias Bay, became unmanned in 1934. This very small island was subject to many violent seas, with the keepers and their families being stranded for many months at a time. Since the island was so small, the tower was part of the keepers dwelling, jutting out of the roof.

It was reported in 1928, that the dwelling was saved by the keeper who threw open all the windows and doors so the sea could pass through the house rather than carry it away. Avery Rock Lighthouse, having been destroyed years ago, has been replaced by a lighted bouy.

Avery Rock Lighthouse is pictured below courtesy of the National Archives, year unknown.

NASH ISLAND

This light is near South Addison at the east side of the mouth of Pleasant Bay. It was built in 1838 and rebuilt in 1873 and automated in 1958. Later it was discontinued and replaced by a lighted bouy.

The 51 foot tower is all that is left. Due to the lack of a keeper's house efforts to place it on the National Register of Historic Places has fallen on deaf ears, as well as efforts to find a volunteer group to maintain the tower.

NARRAGUAGUS (Pond Island)

This nonfunctioning light was built in 1856 and has been privately owned since 1934. It is located on Pond Island in the Narragaugus Bay.

As with Nash Island, it can only be seen by air or boat.

Pictured below is Nash Island Lighthouse before it was replaced by the current lighthouse in 1873. The photograph is courtesy of the National Archives, the year is unknown.

The distance at which a light can be seen in clear weather, not only depends on its candlepower, but also on the curvature of the earth.

PROSPECT HARBOR POINT

This lighthouse is on an active military base and not open to the public. It can however, be easily photographed from Prospect Harbor.

The light was built in 1891 to replace the 1850 lighthouse and is red with white flashes.

To reach Prospect Harbor, take Route 195, turn left by the sign to Corea and go 2/10 of a mile to Fireroad 605, 195 goes to the left, but go straight on FR 605. You will be able to photgraph the light from the shoreline.

WINTER HARBOR

This light, which was built in 1856, is located on Mark Island across Frenchman Bay from Bar Harbor. Under private ownership since 1934, it is no longer a functioning light.

The light can be reached by taking Rt. 186 from US 1 and W. Gouldsboro south to Schoodic Point. Photographs can be taken from the road going around Acadia National Park.

PETIT MANAN

At 123 feet, this is the second tallest lighthouse in Maine and its white flashing light is visible for 26 miles. It was built of granite in 1855, to replace the original 53 foot tower of 1817. It could be said the lighthouse was built twice, first the granite was cut and assembled at a quarry in Trenton, Maine. The stones were numbered, dismantled, brought to the island by boat, and reassembled to build the tower. The island is now managed by the Fish and Wildlife Service; however, the tower, which was unmanned in 1972 is still under the jurisdiction of the Coast Guard.

The light is on the east point of Petit Manan Island, 2 1/2 miles off Petit Manan Point south of Millbridge. This is one of the foggiest locations along the East Coast being engulfed in fog nearly 20 percent of the year.

The light is best photographed by air or boat; however, on clear days, this light can be seen in the distance from the road to Schoodic Point at Arcadia National Park.

Artifacts of Petit Manan Light including the second order lense previously in the tower are proudly on display at the Shore Village Museum in Rockland, Maine.

CRABTREE LEDGE

This spark plug type light was located in Frenchmans Bay, one quarter mile off the easterly shore of Crabtree Neck near the town of Hancock Point. Built in 1890, this lightstation had a fifth order lense, which was visible for 12 miles, and stood 48 feet above the water. It was sold at auction to a private party; it later became structurally unsound and collapsed into the bay in 1934.

The photograph below, courtesy of the National Archives, was taken sometime before 1920.

BEAR ISLAND

Originally built in 1839 and rebuilt in 1889, this light was deactivated in 1982 and was replaced by a lighted bouy. Fortunately, due to public outcry, the Coast Guard recently reactivated the Bear Island Light.

The light marks the entrance to Northeast Harbor on Mt. Desert Island and can be photographed by air or boat. The mail boat out of Norhteast Harbor, which operates year round, offers the best views. During the months of July and August, the tour boats out of Bar Harbor pass close to this light.

BAKER ISLAND

The original light was built in 1828 under orders of President John Quincy Adams. The present light was built in 1855 and is now part of Acadia National Park.

Baker Island Light, situated on an island 123 acres in size, is best photographed by air or boat. The light can also be seen from the summit of Cadillac Mountain.

This 45 foot high tower became automated in 1966.

EGG ROCK

This light was built in 1875 on an exposed island of the foggy Maine Coast, marking the entrance to Frenchman Bay. It is a stubby tower atop the keeper's house with a red flashing light.

The light can be seen by taking Rt. 3 from Ellsworth to Acadia National Park and photographed from one of the scenic overlooks on the eastern side of the park. Tour boats operating out of Bar Harbor between Memorial Day and Columbus Day will give you the opportunity to take excellent close-up photos of the lighthouse.

While in the area, we would highly recommend that you spend the time to drive to the summit of Cadillac Mountain. From the summit, you will be able to see several lighthouses and experience the most extraordinary views anywhere in Maine.

The black and white insert is Egg Rock Light as it appeared in the late 1800's courtesy of Shore Village Museum.

MOUNT DESERT ROCK

A simple look at the charts will prove that this lightstation was the most isolated of all lighthouses along the Maine coast. In even the most mild of storms, waves wash over the entire island. The tiny island, which is only 600 yards long and about 200 yards wide, is located 20 miles south of Mount Desert Island, which was reportedly named by Sameul de Champlain in 1604. The first light at Mt. Desert Rock was in 1830 and consisted of a lantern resting on timbers across the roof of the keepers home, 56 feet above the ocean. Records indicate that in a storm in 1842 a boulder 18 feet long, 14 feet wide, and 6 feet thick, weighing 57 tons was thrown out of its place by waves. During another storm, a 75 ton boulder was moved 60 feet.

In 1857, a new stone tower was erected to a height of 75 feet with a fixed beam until 1898 when it became a flashing white light, which it still is today. The lighthouse, which was automated in 1977, can be photographed only by air or boat, but if attempting to do so, remember the tiny rock is 26 miles from the nearest harbor.

The photograph above is Mount Desert Lightstation as it appeared in the late 1800's, courtesy of the Shore Village Museum, Rockland, Maine.

GREAT DUCK ISLAND

This light was built in 1890 under orders of President Benjaman Harrison. It is 5 1/2 miles southeast of Bass Harbor and can best be photographed by air or boat from the south side of the island.

Although being a remote island, it nad a one teacher school house, built in 1904. Nathan Adam Reed, who served as keeper from 1902 to 1912, had sixteen children that attended this school along with the children of two other keepers.

The island is now owned by the Maine Chapter of the Nature Conservancy, which estimates that this island supports 20 percent of Maine's nesting seabirds.

One of the many tales of the Maine Coast, tells of an amazing story of a dog named Seaboy. Legend has it that during a shipwreck, the dog tried to jump into a lifeboat. However, a fightened crewman, struck the dog with an oar and knocked him into the stormy ocean and it was believed that the dog had drowned. The injured, half-drowned dog made it ashore and was nutured back to health by the daughter of one of the keepers. She named the dog Seaboy and they became inseparable over the next two years. One day the captain of a fishing vessel came to Great Duck Island and enjoyed a happy reunion with the dog he thought had drowned years ago. When it came time for the captain to leave, the keeper's daughter, thinking her pet was lost for sure, cried out as the dog went with the captain. Hearing her cry, the dog jumped out of the dory, and back into the arms of the girl who had saved his life.

The photograph below was taken in 1950 and is courtesy of the United States Coast Guard. Pictured on the opposite page is how Great Duck Island appears today.

BASS HARBOR

(pictured on opposite page)

This light was built in 1858. It is on the southwest point of Mount Desert Island and can easily be reached by car. The residence is private property, however, there are public access trails to the left and right of the light house. Breathtaking pictures can be obtained from these vantage points. This is a truly beautiful area so be prepared to spend some time and take a lot of pictures. Unfortunately, there are no public facilities at this light.

The light can be seen from Maine State Ferries that operate out of Bass Harbor for Swans Island and Frenchboro. By car, take Rt. 3 from Ellsworth to Rt. 198 and turn right, then to Rt. 102 and turn right again to Bass Harbor. There are signs to guide you to the dirt road that leads to the parking lot.

BLUE HILL BAY

Located on Fly Island, this lighthouse was built in 1857, and became private property in 1935. Fly Island is in Blue Hill Bay a few miles north of Swans Island.

As you can see by the photographs, the tower is no higher than the keepers dwelling. Since the island is so flat, its size changes drastically with the changing of the tides. It can only be photographed by air or boat.

BURNT COAT HARBOR/HOCKAMOCK HEAD

Swans Island was named after Colonel James Swan, one of the original Sons of Liberty. Colonel Swan was one of the participants of the Boston Tea Party and he fought for American Independence in the Revolutionary War. Later Colonel Swan tried to set up his own empire at Swans Island; he failed and ended up in a debtors prison in France. Later the island was settled by David Smith who became known as King David. He fathered 24 children and some of his decendents still live on Swans Island.

In 1872 two lighthouses were built on the southwest tip of the island. These lights, known as range lights, were built a distance apart with the rear light at a higher elevation. When the ship's captain lines range lights up, this signals a safe channel. However, the lights must have caused some confusion, because shipwrecks increased in the area. In 1885, the lighthouse board had the smaller light torn down leaving the current lighthouse on Hockamock Head. This light still stands today with its flashing green light.

Swans Island is located several miles from the mainland and can be reached via car ferry out of Bass Harbor. As with all ferry services operating in Maine, be sure to check with schedules, as they may change with demand and you could be stranded on an island indefinately. During peak seasons, you may need reservations for ferry service.

The Lighthouse Service was one of the first public works created by the United States Government. The first session of Congress passed an act on August 7, 1789 providing that all lighthouses would come under the jurisdiction of the U.S. Government and managed by the Treasury Department. Reluctantly the states ceded their lighthouses to the new central Government. Over the years many branches of the government had jurisdiction over lighthouses, with final control now with the U.S. Coast Guard.

SADDLEBACK LEDGE

This light, built in 1839 on a ledge of rocks between Vinalhaven and Isle au Haut, was a desolate place for any keeper. While it was manned, it had an unmistakable reputation for being the most difficult station at which to make a landing. As you can see by our photograph, all traces of the keepers dwelling have been washed away. The island has no soil on it. The keepers had to haul dirt to the island in order to grow vegetables in the cracks of rocks. Winter storms would wash the soil away and in the spring the keepers would have to haul more soil out to the island.

The light is now automated with a white flashing light and can be best seen by air or boat.

Pictured below is Saddleback Ledge Light as it appeared in the late 1800's. Photograph courtesy of the United States Coast Guard.

ISLE AU HAUT

Samuel de Champlain discovered the island in 1604 calling it Isle Haut, meaning high island. The island is located south of Stonington and is part of Acadia National Park.

The light was built in 1907 and is a functioning light. The Keeper's House, which is privately owned and operated as a bed & breakfast, sits atop ragged ledges overlooking the Atlantic, surrounded by dense spruce forests and island panoramas. Now on the National Register of Historic Places, the restored station is a living museum where guests can take a step back in time.

For information and reservations, you may contact them at **The Keeper's House, P.O. Box 26, Isle au Haut, Maine 04645, (207)367-2261.**

The island can be reached by the mail boat from Stonington year round (except Sundays and Postal holidays). For information, call (207)367-5193. The sketch below is courtesy of Jeff & Judi Burke, The Keeper's House, Isle au Haut, Maine.

You can also camp on the island; however, applications must be made by mail far in advance by writing to Acadia National Park, Isle au Haut Reservations, P.O. Box 177, Bar Harbor, Maine 04609.

DEER ISLAND THOROFARE/MARK ISLAND

This light was built in 1857 on the west side of Mark Island guarding the western approach to Deer Island Thorofare and has a white flashing light.

With binoculars, the light tower can be seen from Stonington as well as off of Route 15; although it is best photographed by air or boat.

The photograph below is Deer Island Thorofare Lightstation as it appeared some time in the late 1800's, courtesy of the Shore Village Museum, Rockland, Maine.

PUMPKIN ISLAND LIGHT

This light, built in 1854, is no longer a functioning light and is privately owned.

The light is at the northern part of Eggemoggin Reach. To photograph this light, take Rt. 15 over the Deer Island suspension bridge, stay to the right of the information booth and turn right onto the gravel road just past it to a parking area where you will be able to get good photographs.

EAGLE ISLAND

This light is located on Eagle Island between Deer Isle and North Haven in Penobscot Bay. This lighthouse, which is still functioning, was built in 1858, replacing the original light of 1839. In an unfortunate economy blunder, the keeper's quarters and other buildings were demolished by the Coast Guard in 1963.

Eagle Island, rich in history and in beauty, can be only reached by boat or air. *A Family Island in Penobscot Bay* by John C. Enk and Erland L. Quinn gives a good representation of life on Eagle Island.

DICE HEAD

This lighthouse is located in the beautiful and historic village of Castine. One of the oldest towns in America, it is at the entrance to the Penobscot River. The village was named after the wealthy and adventurous Baron de St. Castine, who took over the town in 1676.

Because the coastal village was an extremely strategic location, the flags of France, England, and the Netherlands as well as the United States, have flown here. During the Revolution, Paul Revere led an army of patriots in an unsuccessful attack against Fort George.

By the time of the War of 1812, the U.S. had built Fort Madison at this location. The fort was lost to the British, who held the town until the end of the war.

The light, which is no longer a functioning light, was built in 1828, rebuilt in 1858, and again in 1937. At one time the tower was octagonal in shape.

To reach Dice Head Light, take Rt 175 south from Orland to Rt 166 past Fort George, go past the Maine Maritime Academy to where the road turns into Battle Ave. You will see the light from there, but for some great views of the light and the area, there is a public path to your left, by the garage.

While in the area, be sure to tour the ruins of Fort Madison and Fort George.

FORT POINT

This light was built under orders from President Andrew Jackson in 1836, and was renovated in 1857. The fog bell house, one of the last of its kind, still stands.

At the light, be sure to tour the ruins of Ft. Pownall, which was a French fort, established in 1759 during the French and Indian Wars.

Two battles were also fought here during the Revolution. This was the sight of a famous sea and land battle, where 1000 Patriots under the command of Colonel Paul Revere and Commodore Dudley Saltonstall fled the British and lost 43 ships.

The light is easy to find and you will be able to take photographs from many different angles. From Stockton Springs, take East Cape Road past the entrance to Ft. Point State Park and the left to a small dirt parking lot.

GRINDLE POINT

Grindle Point Light was built in 1850, improved 1874, unmanned in 1934 and now has been reactivated by the Coast Guard. The keepers dwelling now houses the Islesboro Sailor's Memorial Museum.

This light which is located on the north side of the entrance to Gilkey Harbor, can be seen from the ferry landing at Lincolnville. To get to the lighthouse, simply take the auto ferry from Lincolnville to Islesboro Island, however, there is no need to bring your car as the lighthouse is at the ferry landing. To verify the ferry scedule, call (207)789-5611.

CURTIS ISLAND

This light which marks the south side entrance to Camden Harbor, is located on Curtis Island, which was named after Cyrus Curtis who was publisher of the Saturday Evening Post. The tower with its fixed green light was built in 1896, replacing the original tower of 1838.

This light is best photographed by boat or plane. The Town of Camden operates the area as a public park accessible only by private boat.

To view this light by car, take US 1 in Camden turn south on Chestnut Street in front of the Camden Post Office, proceed to Penobscot Ave. and turn left, bear left at the small barricade and you will be able to see the light to your left. There is no parking in this area, but you may be able to make a quick stop in the street to take a picture.

GOOSE ROCK

Goose Rock Light, resembling a spark plug, is located between Vinalhaven and North Haven Islands. It was built in 1890 and automated in 1963.

The keepers were confined to a few small rooms in the tower, and there was obviously no room for families.

The light is best photographed by air or boat, but can be seen from a distance from Vinalhaven Island.

INDIAN ISLAND

Originally built in 1875 this light was sold in 1933 and is now privately owned.

It is located at the eastern end of Rockport Harbor and can be seen from the Rockport Marine Park. From US 1 in Rockport, turn onto Main St. by Rocknaks Yacht Sales, go to the bridge and turn right. The sign for the park will be on your left. This park has picnic tables for your enjoyment.

BROWNS HEAD

Built in 1857, this light replaced the original of 1832, and is located on the northwest point of Vinalhaven Island. To reach the lighthouse, take the Rockland Ferry to Vinalhaven. Be sure to call (207) 594-5543 to verify ferry departures times, so you don't get stranded on the island overnight.

This lighthouse is very difficult to find on your own, as most of the roads on the island are unmarked. The residents of Vinalhaven are known for their friendliness, so feel free to ask for directions or try to find a tour guide.

Our special thanks to local resident Randy Farnham, who gave us a ride to the lighthouse and informative tour of Vinalhaven Island.

HERON NECK

Built in 1854 on Green Island, it is southwest of Carvers Harbor near Vinalhaven. In 1989 an apparent electrical fire nearly destroyed the keeper's dwelling, however the tower with its functioning light was undamaged.

Presently, the Coast Guard is looking for someone to repair and maintain this station. The costs of restoration are estimated to be well over $300,000.00.

Recently, the owner of Green Island renamed it Bush Island in honor of President George Bush.

Heron Neck Light can only be viewed by air or boat.

Pictured below is Heron Neck Lighthouse as it appeared in 1937, courtesy of the United States Coast Guard.

ROCKLAND - CAMDEN AREA

Rockland is rich in its history to the sea as is evident by its fishing industry, which has played an important role in the survival of the local economy. Its busy harbor supports hundreds of Lobster Boats, a commercial fishing fleet, windjammers, yachts, deep sea fishing boats, sightseeing boats, sail boats, the state ferrries, and the United States Coast Guard which maintains a permanent base here.

Rockland, stated to be the Lobster Capitol of the World, is the home of The Maine Lobster Festival held every August, which attracts people from all over the world.

Rockland's business district which is within walking distance to the harbor is listed in the National Register of Historic Places.

The Shore Village Museum, probably the best Lighthouse Museum in the world is also located here and is a must see for any lighthouse enthusiast.

If you have ever wanted to visit Cabot Cove of "Murder She Wrote" fame, we would suggest a visit to the beautiful coastal village of Camden, Maine. Camden is reputed to be the yacht capital of the world, and its harbor dotted with vessels of all shapes and sizes, is one of the most photographic anywhere.

Three miles from Camden off US 1, is Camden Hills State Park. The park has 5,000 picturesque acres and offers excellent summer picnicking and camping with a rugged shoreline setting. Once in the park, you can hike or drive to the top of Mount Battie where there is an observation tower offering breathtaking views of Penobscot Bay

If you are a true lighthouse enthusiast you might want to stay at the Lighthouse Motel, which is located off Rte. 1, four and a half miles north of Camden and overlooking Penobscot Bay and Grindle Point Lighthouse in the distance. The Lighthouse Motel is said to have the largest private collection of Maine lighthouse paintings anywhere. They are open April to October and reservations are a must, call them at (207)236-2758.

The nearby coastal communities of Rockport, Port Clyde, Tenants Harbor, Thomaston, and Fort George are also rich in maritime history and are well worth visiting.

ROCKLAND BREAKWATER

Built in 1902, replacing the original light of 1888, this light is located in Rockland Harbor, extending nearly a mile out from Jameson's Point.

This functioning light has recently undergone extensive and costly Coast Guard renovations.

From US 1 turn onto Waldo Rd (by the Baptist church) to Samoset Road and turn right. Samoset Road dead ends to a small parking area. A short walk will bring you to the breakwater where you can walk the 7/8 of a mile out to the lighthouse. To obtain beautiful sunrise photographs of the light, take US 1 to Falls St. to the end. This will get the lighthouse and sun lined up perfectly for great early morning pictures.

The Maine State Ferry out of Rockland to Vinalhaven passes close to Rockland Breakwater Light as well as the nearby Owls Head Light.

ROCKLAND HARBOR SOUTHWEST

Have you ever wanted to build your own lighthouse? Well, lighthouse enthusiast Bruce Woollet did and it was completed in 1985. Through the assistance and support of Ken Black of the Shore Village Museum in Rockland, Mr. Woollet was able to obtain a license and in November, 1987 it became an official Coast Guard lighthouse.

Rockland Harbor Southwest Lighthouse can be photographed from various points on Rt 73 and North Shore Drive on the way to or from Owls Head Lighthouse.

THE SHORE VILLAGE MUSEUM

MAINE'S LIGHTHOUSE MUSEUM

104 Limerock Street

Rockland, Maine 04841

If you are truly a lighthouse buff, or even a novice just getting interested in the historic part lighthouses and their keepers played in the growing up of America, the Shore Village Museum is a place you must visit.

The Lighthouse Museum, which is the brainchild of former Coast Guardsman Ken Black, is housed in the Grand Army Hall, a building which was donated by the Daughters of Union Veterans. The museum is reported to have the largest collection of lighthouse artifacts anywhere in the nation. There are literally hundreds of items on display, including but not limited to, lifesaving equipment, nautical instruments, photographs, Civil War Naval materials, and lighthouse collectors cards. The foghorns, bells, and lenses on display are all in excellent working order. While touring the museum, you will be able to view the large and impressive second-order Fresnel lense, which was built for Petit Manan Lighthouse.

There is a great gift shop that has post cards of hundreds of lighthouses, lighthouse books and calenders, and other various lighthouse gift items.

The Shore Village Musum is open free to the public daily June 1 to October 15 from 10 am to 4 pm and they furnish a informative guided tour or you can browse on your own. The museum is also open year round by appointment to interested tour groups.

Pictured above is Ken "Mr. Lighthouse" Black with the third order fresnel lense which was originally installed at Whitehead Light, St. George, Maine

To become a member of the museum and receive their lighthouse newsletter write to them at:

The Shore Village Historical Society

c/o John Venskus, Treasurer

SR32, Box 99

Owls Head, Maine 04854

Membership dues are as follows:

Regular Membership - $5.00

Family (husband, wife, and children under 18) - $8.00

Sustaining Member - $50.00

Organization Member - $25.00

Junior Members $1.00

Senior Citizens - $2.00

Pictured above is the Grand Army Hall in Rockland Maine, which houses the Shore Village Lighthouse Museum.

Pictured at left are lighthouse collectors' cards from Hassan Cork Tip Cigarettes, which in its time claimed to be the largest selling brand of cigarettes in the United States. A large collection of lighthouse cards is on display at the Shore Village Museum.

OWLS HEAD

In September of 1825, Keeper Isaac Stearns illuminated Owls Head Light for the first time.

Although the short, stubby tower is only 20 feet tall, it stands a magnificent 100 feet above the water.

You can reach light by taking US 1 in Rockland to Route 73, proceed to North Shore Drive and turn left, go about 2 1/2 miles and turn left by the old Owls Head Post Office onto Main Street, to Lighthouse Road and turn left. Lighthouse Road will become a dirt road then bear right to the parking area. A short walk will bring you to the lighthouse. No matter what the season or the weather, this area is a photographer's dream; however, be careful with small children as there are many cliffs with straight drops to the ocean below.

Owls Head Light which is on the National Register of Historic Places, can also be viewed from the state ferries operating out of Rockland.

Check with your library for Edward Snow's **Famous Lighthouses of New England** which recounts interesting tales and acts of heroism associated with Owls Head Lighthouse.

TWO BUSH ISLAND

Located outside the west side of Penobscot Bay, this light was built in 1897 and automated in 1964.

Since no one could be found to take over the buildings, the government had the Green Berets blow up the keepers house in a demolition exercise. This is just one more reason why the American public should be more active in the preservation of landmarks.

The light can only be photographed by air or boat.

WHITE HEAD

This lighthouse was built under orders of President Thomas Jefferson in 1807 and rebuilt in 1852. It is located on a small island near Tenants Harbor marking the entrance to Muscle Ridge Channel. Due to the fact that the area is covered with fog an average of one out of every five days, a perpetual fog bell was installed in 1837. This was the first successful attempt to harness the power of the ocean for this purpose. The rise and fall of the tide wound a weight-operated spring mechanism that drove a striking mechanism, thus operating the fog signal continually.

In 1805, two shipwrecked sailors froze to death on the island and their remains were not found until the following Spring. To this day their graves are still on the island.

The lightstation can be photographed by air or boat.

TENANTS HARBOR

Tenants Harbor Lighthouse was built in 1857 and sold privately on December 27, 1933. The non functioning light is located on Southern Island and can be seen from Tenants Harbor by turning left at the East Wind Inn and following the shoreline where you can obtain a good view.

MARSHALL POINT

The light was built in 1832 and replaced in 1857. The keeper's house is now a museum, restored by the St. George Historical Society and administered by the Maine Historic Preservation Society. Marshall Point Lighthouse can be reached by taking US 1 to Thomaston to Rt 131 south to Port Clyde. Turn left at the main intersection, then right immediately beyond the restaurant onto the paved but unmarked Marshall Point Road. Proceed one mile to the lighthouse parking lot.

The black and white insert shows the enclosed walkway during the early 1900's, courtesy of Shore Village Museum.

MATINICUS ROCK

Mantinicus Rock is a 30 acre barren rock about six miles south of Matinicus Island which is 25 miles from Rockland. The light guards the entrance to Penobscot Bay. It was a lonely isolated station for keepers and most did not stay on very long.

Over the years, there have been many cases of heroism credited to the keepers of Matinicus Rock, of which many are credited to Abbie Burgess. Upon the death of her two year old daughter in 1881, Abbie Burgess by scraping together a few handfulls of dirt, buried her baby between the ledges and then erected a wooden cross. Nearly one hundred years later, Harriet and Carl Buchheister hired a mason to carve a headstone which with the assistance of the Coast Guard, was placed on the island. Abbie Burgess and her husband Isaac Grant who served as keepers at Matinicus Rock Light also served at White Head Lightstation for fifteen years. Many years after Abbie Burgess-Grant was dead and buried, her dream to have a tombstone in the form of a lighthouse came true. A replica of a lighthouse beacon was placed on her grave by famous lighthouse historian Edward Rowe Snow.

The island has been the target of many violent storms. The first lighthouses were built in 1827 and consisted of two wooden towers. On Sunday, January 27, 1839 a violent storm forced the keeper and his family to flee the island and the two towers were demolished. Two more wooden towers were built and were then replaced by two stone towers in 1848. Again the towers suffered damage from storms and had to be torn down and replaced by granite towers in 1857. These towers still stand today. The lantern room has been removed from one of the towers leaving only one functioning light on this desolate rock.

Frank Hilt, keeper from 1919 to 1928, scored a journalistic coup when in 1923 he heard of President Warren Harding's death on his radio. He called the Rockland Courier Gazette for details only to learn that they had not yet heard of the President's passing.

The light which is visible for 23 miles became unmanned in December. It is best photographed by air or boat.

If you cannot make it to the island to see the towers, the 1800 pound fog bell can be seen at the Shore Village Museum in Rockland.

The photograph below is Matinicus Rock Light as it appeared in the 1890's courtesy of the United States Coast Guard.

MATINCUS ROCK LIGHT during 1983 automation. Photographs courtesy of Bob Davis, Rockland Maine.

Abbie Burgess-Grant's grave at Forest Hill Cemetary

MANANA ISLAND FOG STATION

In 1854, a 2500 pound fog bell was installed at Monhegan Island Light; however, sailors complained that they could not hear the bell, so a fog signal station was built in 1870 on Manana Island. The fog station is still active today. The picture above is Manana Island Fog Station as it appeared in the late 1800's, courtesy of Shore Village Museum.

The following individual is trying to archive fog signal recordings. If you have access to any of these recordings or know where any of them can be obtained, you may contact Jeff Laser, 4 McGibeny # J-4, Mt. Vernon, Ohio 43056.

MONHEGAN ISLAND

Since Monhegan Island was the first point sighted in most trans-Atlantic voyages, it was the logical place for this lighthouse. The light was first lit July 2, 1824.

Monhegan Island was originally settled in 1614 as a haven from Indians and is considered Maine's earliest fishing village. John Smith orignally named the island *Barties* and a monument on the island perpetuates his name there. He was not successful in keeping the name for the island and few people other than historians have ever heard of it as Barties Island. The actual name probably comes from the Indian word monhegan which translates as *the island.*

The famous pirate Dixey Bull was active in this area before his capture and execution. In the War of 1812, a famous sea battle was fought between the **Boxer** and the **Enterprise**. On September 5, 1814, the people of Monhegan Island gathered on a high bluff to watch the sea battle which took place between Mohegan Island and Port Clyde. The battle which ended with an American victory and the death of both captains, was immortilized in Longfellow's poem *My Lost Youth.*

The 47 foot tall tower is 178 feet above the water being located on high ground on the island. Monhegan Island can be reached by air or boat from Port Clyde. From mid June to mid September the Balmy Days tour boat out of Boothbay Harbor goes to the Island. Year round accessibility is available through the mail boat the *Laura B* out of Port Clyde (207)372-8848. There are tourist accommodations on the island.

In 1959, when the light was automated, the keeper's dwellings were turned into a museum.

The photograph is courtesy of the United States Coast Guard.

FRANKLIN ISLAND

Franklin Island Light was constructed in 1855 to replace a daymarker built in 1805. The light was automated in 1967 and the keeper's house and other dwellings were dismantled by the Coast Guard. It is located on the northwest side of Franklin Island in Muscongus Bay.

It can only be reached by air or boat. If you wish to photograph the tower, you may be able to rent or charter a boat in the village of Friendship.

The black and white photograph above is courtesy of the United States Coast Guard, and was how Franklin Island once appeared.

PEMAQUID POINT

This is truly one of the prettiest lighthouses in all of Maine and maybe all of New England and the spot is a photographer's dream come true.

The lighthouse, originally built in 1827 and rebuilt in 1857, is 38 feet tall but sits a lofty 79 feet above the water.

The people of Bristol maintain the interesting and informative Fishermen's Museum here as well as ample parking and picnic tables. The museum has artifacts of Maine lighthouses and the fishing and lobster industry.

The rocks below the lighthouse which you can climb and relax on are the most unique and colorful on the Maine coast.

Next door to the lighthouse, is the Sea Gull Giftshop and Restaurant where you can enjoy a snack or meal with breathtaking views overlooking the ocean and rocks below.

To get to this picturesque lighthouse, take US 1 to Damariscotta and then south on Rt. 130 which ends at Pemaquid Point. Tour boats out of Boothbay Harbor also pass by this light.

This is one location you definately must see as no other location along the Maine coast can compare to the majestic beauty of Pemaquid Point.

DOUBLING POINT

Doubling Point Lighthouse was built in 1898. It can been seen from across the river by taking Washington Street, which becomes Webber Road, in Bath past **Bath Iron Works** (home of the finest shipbuilders in the world) on the way to Rt 209 toward Phippsburg.

While in this area, we would encourage you to visit the Maine Maritime Museum, which is located at 243 Washington Street in Bath. The museum's artifacts include paintings, ship models, navigational instruments, as well as a large collection of boats. You can explore the shipyard, where many of the most famous schooners of all time were built, watch boatbuilders at work, and enjoy a picnic on the grounds. For more information, you may call them at (207)443-1316.

SQUIRREL POINT

Completed in 1898, Squirrel Point Light is located on the southwest point of Arrowsic Island.

To reach the light by land, from Woolrich take Rt 127 toward Arrowsic. Turn right onto Steen Road then right again onto Bald Head Road (which is a dirt road) to a small parking area. From there you will walk a little under a mile along the footpath to the light. There are several paths leading from the parking area, listen for the sound of the water to find the right direction. You will go over a small foot bridge and then follow the marked path through the woods to the light.

It can also be viewed from across the river on Rt. 209 between Phippsburg and Bath.

KENNEBEC RIVER/DOUBLING POINT RANGE LIGHTS

These towers built in 1908, are two wooden towers, with the rear tower being 235 yards behind the tower on shore. Their lights are lined up in such a way as to show the middle of the river channel to a vessel.

To reach this lighthouse take US 1 to Rt 127 south to a dirt road marked Doubling Point Road, and left at the fork marked Kennebec River Light.

BOOTHBAY HARBOR REGION

The Boothbay Harbor Region is truly a boaters and tourist paradise. No matter where you go in the Boothbay Harbor area, you will find great gift shops, antique stores, unusual and quaint Bed & Breakfast Inns, harbor view motels, and friendly people in a photographic environment.

The seasons never stop here, starting with the Fisherman's Festival in early spring, Windjammer Days in June, blue fish and tuna tournaments in August, the Fall Foliage Festival, and the Arrival of Santa Claus by boat at Christmas.

There are tourboats galore with over 50 harbor cruises every day (some going past up to six lighthouses), and seafood prepared at it best offered everywhere.

You might also consider a visit to the Oceans East Aquarium & Living Museum of the Gulf of Maine on Pier 30, Atlantic Ave in Boothbay Harbor. Be sure to call them for hours at (207)633-3965.

For more information on the Boothbay Area we suggest you write the Boothbay Harbor Region Chamber of Commerce at P.O. Box 356, Boothbay Harbor, Maine 04538 or call them at (207)633-2353.

Burnt Island Lighthouse, Boothbay Harbor

RAM ISLAND

This light built in 1883 is on Ram Island on the eastern side of Boothbay Harbor.

The island has picnic areas and the Grand Banks Schooner Museum.

It can photographed by taking US 1 to Route 27 to Route 96 East to Ocean Point. There is a small parking area there where you can take photographs of the light from a distance. However, as with most of the lights in this area, it is best photographed from one of the tour boats out of Boothbay Harbor.

BURNT ISLAND

This light was built in 1821 and altered in 1888. Located on the west side of the entrance Boothbay Harbor, it can be seen from the east side of the harbor, however, it is best photographed from one of the tour boats operating out of Boothbay Harbor.

SEQUIN ISLAND

Originally built in 1795 from orders of President Washington at a cost of $6300, this was a wooden tower which was replaced in 1820 with a new stone tower. In 1857, a new tower was built and for the first time in Maine, a first order Fresnel lense was placed in a lantern of a tower. Although the tower is only 53 feet tall, it is the highest above water in all in all of Maine at 186 feet. On a clear day, the light can be seen at a distance of 40 miles.

In 1936, to squelch rumors of buried treasure on Sequin Island, the Bureau of Lighthouses hired a man to spend a full year searching for the treasure. After only nine months of searching, he proclaimed the island to be free of treasure.

The lighthouse which is located at the mouth of the Kennebec River can be photographed from one of the tour boats out of Boothbay Harbor. To view by car, take Rt 209 from US 1 in Bath to Popham Beach, where you can see the lighthouse in the distance.

POND ISLAND

Also near Popham Beach, this light was built in 1821 and rebuilt in 1855, and became unmanned in 1963. Sadly, all that remains today is the tower.

Although best seen by air or boat, Pond Island Light can be viewed from Highway 209 and along the road to Fort Popham. The light is far off shore so be sure to bring your binoculars along.

PERKINS ISLAND

Built in 1898 on the eastern side of the Kennebec River near the village of Parker Head, this light can be easily photographed from across the river.

To reach the light take Rt 209 from US 1 to Phippsburg, just past the Phippsburg Post Office turn left by the Phippsburg General Store and Irving Gas onto the road marked MR40. The sign is small and located on a telephone pole so be prepared. The road will follow the river to the village of Parker Head where you will be able to see the lighthouse.

THE CUCKOLDS

In 1907 the light was added to a fog signal house. It was automated and unmanned in 1975. The original fourth order lens is on display at the Shore Village Museum in Rockland.

Located on a small island in Boothbay Harbor near the village of Newagen, it can be seen off Rt. 27 south from US 1 to the town landing. It can also be photographed from one of the tour boats out of Boothbay Harbor.

HENDRICKS HEAD

Built in 1875, this light replaced the original light of 1829. The lighthouse is located on Southport Island on the east side of the mouth of the Sheepscot River. Off Rt. 27 in Southport take the third road intersection (similar to a rotary) and go to the beach road. The light will appear on your left. Although it is private property, good photographs can be taken from the beach.

The following account was reported by keeper Charles Knight who served between the first and second World Wars. One night he went to mail a letter and encoutered a woman walking in the opposite direction. This puzzled him as he wondered what she was doing walking in that lonely section of Southport after dark. However he did not stop to speak with her. When he arrived at the post office the postmaster had also stated that he had seen the unidentified woman. The next day when the tide had gone out her drowned body was found weighted down with a flatiron. Her identity was never known and she was buried in Southport.

Even to this day people in the vicinity claim she returns to haunt the beach where she committed suicide, and there are some who claim they have seen her ghostly figure walking the deserted beach in the winter months.

LIGHTSHIP NANTUCKET # 112

At one time there were some 70 lightships stationed off the coast of the United States, with the first lightship being stationed off Cheasapeake Bay in 1820. Lightships were placed where it was impractical to build a lighthouse and they could be moved as conditions changed.

A lightship blown or dragged from its station and not showing its lights or sounding its foghorn could spell disaster for an unsuspecting vessel.

A cabinet official in the early 1930's is quoted as saying, **"The Government has a fleet of vessels in its service whose duty it is to go where no other vessels are allowed to go and through storms, darkness and sunshine, do their work for humanity without any boasting, without any advertising, with none to trumpet their praises."** Sound familiar? The statement sounds like something of a cross between Star Trek and the old Postal Service. All kidding aside, records and published accounts indicate and tell of the many brave deeds and acts of heroism by the crews of lightships.

In October 1916 before the United States entered the First World War, a raid by a German submarine sank 6 vessels in the area of Nantucket. The crews of these sunken ships were rescued by Lightship Nantucket # 85 and at one time there were 115 shipwrecked sailors on board. Had it not been for the lightship these men would probably have drowned in the stormy seas that followed the German raid.

In 1934, in a heavy fog in the area of Nantucket Shoals the British liner OLYMPIC (sister ship of the TITANIC) rammed and sank the Lightship Nantucket # 117 with a loss of 7 of its 11 man crew. The Olympic's owners paid to have a replacement ship built which is the LIGHTSHIP NANTUCKET # 112 pictured here.

The Lightship Nantucket # 112 served in the Nantucket Shoals area, and during WW II it was fitted with guns and used to guard the harbor area. In 1975 the Coast Guard decommissioned the lightship.

The LIGHTSHIP NANTUCKET # 112 now designated a **National Historic Landmark** is open to the public as a floating museum located at the Main Wharf next to the Casco Bay Ferry Terminal in Portland Maine.

Whatever your level of interest the volunteer organization that manages the lightship is always looking for new members. You may write them at Lightship Nantucket # 112, 58 Fore Street, Portland, Maine 04101, or call them at (207)775-1181.

PORTLAND MAINE

Portland, originally named Falmouth was first settled in 1632 by the British as a fishing and trading settlement.

The town had its difficulties in growing since it was burned to the ground three different times. The first time being in 1675, when it was completely burned by an Indian attack. Falmouth was resettled and by the early 1700's was a flourishing fishing and trading settlement. In 1775, during the Revolutionary War the town was bombarded by a British fleet and most of the buildings were either destroyed or severly damaged by the fires that followed. When the Revolutionary War was over, the town was rebuilt and in 1786 the name was changed to Portland.

Portland, with its great harbor access flourished again with the fishing and shipping industry as well as manufacturing. However, disaster struck again. Caused by fireworks on July 4, 1866, what became known as the GREAT FIRE, flames swept through the city destroying much of Portland and leaving over 10,000 people homeless.

Today Portland is a true seaport metropolis, blending in the old with the new.

Matched only by San Fransico, Portland has over 300 places to eat, from cafes, pubs, bistros, a floating restaurant, and classical dining establishments, with all being reasonably priced.

While in Portland, you might want to visit the WADSWORTH-LONGFELLOW HOUSE. Home of lighthouse lover and poet Henry Wadsworth-Longfellow, the museum is open to the public from June to October, for exact times you may call them at (207)772-1807 or (207)774-1822.

If time permits a stop at the Eastern Promenade, a 68 acre park on the east end of Portland will offer you a beautiful view of Portland Harbor and Casco Bay.

For further information contact the Convention & Visitors Bureau of Greater Portland, 142 Free Street, Portland, Maine 04101. (207)772-4994.

The original steam-powered Lightship Nantucket #112, as it appeared in 1936, the year it was first launched. Photograph is courtesy of the Lightship Nantucket Inc.

PORTLAND BREAKWATER/PETROLEUM DOCKS
"Bug Light"

This lighthouse was built in 1875 replacing the original of 1855. The lighttower of unusual design created to resemble a fourth century greek monument, was originally nearly a mile out on the breakwater. The light, which is on the National Register of Historic Places, was automated in 1935.

During WWII the government filled in the area to provide dry docks in which to build ships for the war. Since the breakwater was gone the light became obsolete and was extinguished in June of 1942.

In 1990, funds were made available from the Maine Historic Preservation Conmission, the South Portland/Cape Elizabeth Rotary Club and the Bicentenial Lighthouse Fund through the National Park Service, to give this light a $26,000 face lift. The restoration project included structural repairs and a fresh coat of paint. Plans are now underway to make a public park in this area.

To reach the lighthouse take Rt 77 from South Portland to Broadway, go east on Broadway to Pickett St. and left on Pickett and follow the road around the warehouses. This light can also be photographed from the tour boats out of Portland. The black and white photograph, showing Bug Light with its keepers quarters is courtesy of the Shore Village Museum.

LITTLE DIAMOND ISLAND OBSERVATORY
"Old Bug Light"

Built in 1855, this was the original **Portland Breakwater Lighthouse.** In 1875, when a new cast iron tower was built, the lighthouse was deactivated and moved to Little Diamond Island in Portland Harbor, between Peaks Island and Portland. It became known as Little Diamond Island Observatory and served as a Lighthouse Service Bouy Depot.

The photographed below, taken in the late 1800's on Diamond Island, is courtesy of the National Archives.

THE PORTLAND OBSERVATORY

Built in 1807 by Captain Lemeul Moody, this structure was built on Portland's highest point, Munjoy Hill, to announce the ships entering Portland Harbor. The 102 steps lead to a breathtaking view of the city, the White Mountains, and of Casco Bay.

It is located at 138 Congress Street in Portland. The Observatory opens to the public in June, Friday through Sunday 1 pm to 5 pm; July through Labor Day, Wednesday through Sunday 1 pm to 5 pm and Saturday 10 am to 5 pm; and September through October it is open weekends only, weather permitting. To verify times call (207)774-5561.

SPRING POINT LEDGE

This lighthouse built in 1897 was originally surrounded by water, until in 1951 when a 900 foot breakwater, using 50,000 tons of granite, was built from shore to the lighttower. The light was powered by kerosene until it was converted to electricty in 1934.

The lighthouse is easily accessible by car and is located in the old Fort Preble area of South Portland, on the west side of the channel to Portland.

To reach this lighthouse take Rt 77, go east on Broadway to Pickett Street and turn right; go to the end of Pickett and turn left onto Fort Road which ends at Fort Preble.

You can walk the breakwater to the lighthouse where you will be able to enjoy the pleasant view of Portland Harbor, Casco Bay, and the Portland skyline. While here you be sure to tour the ruins of Fort Preble as well as a visit to Spring Point Museum. This museum collects and preserves items of historical significance of the Portland Area. Its prized artifact is the recovered bow of the **Snow Squall**, the only surviving American Clipper Ship in the world. The museum's hours vary with the season, you may wish to call them at (209)799-6337.

Although this is a large and beautiful park, beware, there are no public washrooms.

PORTLAND HEAD

Portland Head Light is considered by many to be the patriarch of Maine lighthouses and is probably the most photographed and painted lighthouse in the nation.

Construction began in 1787 under supervision of the Commonwealth of Massachussetts of which Maine was a part of at that time. Construction was taken over by the Federal Government and the lighthouse was believed to be finished in 1790. However officials decided it needed to be taller and Portland Head Light was finally completed in 1791, at a height of 80 feet from the ground and 101 feet from mean high water. The lantern was illuminated for the first time on January 10, 1791, by its first keeper Captain Joseph Greenleaf, who was appointed by President Washington.

Portland Head has been the sight of many shipwrecks, one of those being in February 1864 when the ship **Bohemian** sunk, one of its survivors was John E. Fitzgerald, maternal grandfather of President John F. Kennedy. While visiting Portland Head Light you will note the marker painted on the rocks in memory of the ship the **Annie C. Maguire** which was shipwrecked here on Christmas Eve 1886.

The Coast Guard put on a grand affair for the automation ceremonies on August 7, 1989, linking the automation with the National Lighthouse Day.

During the recent renovation of the keeper's quarters, two port hole windows were discovered that had been covered up and forgotten years ago. The town of Cape Elizabeth will now operate the keeper's quarters as a museum.

At this beautiful park with its panoramic views you will be able to get an exceptionally good view of Ram Island Ledge Light as well as other Portland area lighthouses which are visible in the distance. You can stroll through the spacious park with its rolling hills and ledges, as did Henry Wadsworth-Longfellow in another time and era.

Ample time should be allotted to tour the ruins of Fort Williams, a major army installation dating before the Spanish-American War. During the First and Second World Wars, Fort Williams was the most heavily guarded and fortified military port in the Continental United States.

During the summer many festivals are held here, and picnic tables and washroom facilities are available for your use. The park is open year round including holidays.

To reach the light take Rt. 77 to Cottage Road east which becomes Shore Road to Ft Williams State Park. It can also be photographed from tour boats operating out of Portland.

PORTLAND HEAD LIGHT DURING 1990 RENOVATIONS

RAM ISLAND LEDGE

At high tide the ledges are covered and unseen, and caused many shipwrecks, thus creating the need for a lighthouse on this location. Ram Island Ledge Lighthouse, built in 1905, is about 77 feet high and sits on the jagged rocks at the north side of the entrance to Portland Harbor. It was converted from kerosene to electricty in 1958 and then unmanned in 1959.

It can easily be seen and photographed from Portland Head Light.

THE WRECK OF THE ANNIE C. McGUIRE AT PORTLAND HEAD LIGHT, DECEMBER 24, 1886.

Photograph courtesy of the Maine Historical Society.

HALFWAY ROCK

It took 30 years of debate before funds were appropriated in 1869 to build a lighthouse on this three acre barren rock halfway between Cape Elizabeth and Small Point. The light was finally illuminated on August 15, 1871.

Rough seas and storms are hard on this lighthouse waves often sweeping over the entire island.

An account of a visit to the lighthouse in 1885 describes the interior of the lighthouse, "At the base of the tower was a storeroom, then a circular iron stairway leading to the kitchen. The next flight of stairs brought you to the bedroom of the principle keeper, and above this was a second bedroom with two beds for the assistant keepers. The fourth set of stairs brought you to the watchroom where the keepers stayed on duty all night to make sure the light did not go out. The fifth staircase led you to the lantern room at the top of the tower."

Halfway Rock Light can only by photographed by air or boat, however on a clear day in late afternoon, it can be seen from Portland Head as the sun reflects off the tower.

In 1822, the French physicist Augustin Fresnel revolutionized the lighthouse when he developed a built up annular lens with a central spherical lens surrounded by rings of glass prisms, the central portions which refract and the outer portions both reflect and refract in the desired direction of the light from a single lamp placed at the central focus.

Early lighthouses were illuminated by a variety of oils such as fish oil, sperm oil, colza oil, lard oil, and kerosene.

CAPE ELIZABETH/TWO LIGHTS

A monument 40 feet high with a 20 foot base was first erected at this location in 1811 to serve as a daymarker to mariners. The lighttowers at Cape Elizabeth were first illuminated in October 1828. In 1865 the West Tower was painted with one broad vertical red stripe and the East Tower was given 4 horizontal bands of red, this being done for daytime recognition. Weather and time took their toll and both towers were dismantled and replaced by the current two towers in 1873. Both towers are 67 feet high and 129 feet above water. The beacon in the still functioning east tower is four million candle power, the most powerful of its kind on the New England Coast.

In 1873, Civil War hero and Congressional Medal of Honor recipient Marcus Hanna, bacame the keeper of Two Lights. He was also awarded a gold medal for his rescue of two men from the schooner **Australia** which shipwrecked at Dyers Ledge at Two Lights in a storm in January 1885.

When it was announced by the government in the 1920's that the west tower was to be dismantled, many people protested, however the government was determined. The west tower was discontinued in 1924 and today the west tower and both homes are privately owned. At one time actor Gary Merrill, husband of actress Bette Davis, owned the west tower.

In 1970, Two Lights became the first lighthouse ever pictured on a US Postage Stamp, from a painting by Edward Hopper.

To reach Cape Elizabeth Light, take Rt 77 to Two Lights Road, stay to the left to reach the lighthouse or to the right to reach Two Lights State Park. The beautiful 41 acre park is open to the public from April 15 to November 1 and has picnic areas and trails.

WOOD ISLAND

Wood Island Island was built in 1808 on the east end of Wood Island marking the entrance to the Saco River.

Once the scene of a murder, the island is stated by some to be haunted by the ghost of the victim. In 1896, while drunk a squatter and some-times lobsterman shot and killed a local part-time law officer. He then proceeded to turn himself in to the light keeper. The keeper, frightened by the armed, drunken man with a rifle in his hand, told him to turn himself in to the police. The squatter then proceeded back to his shack and committed suicide. Legend has it that the island is haunted to this day by the ghost of the murdered law officer.

To photograph Wood Island Light take Rt 111 toward Biddeford Pool to Rt 208 South, go past Hatties and bear right past the fire station 1/2 mile to the parking area by the ocean. Look for the fence, where you will find a opening that will take you by foot down the Audobon Trail along the edge of the golf course. A short distance later you will be able to see the light across the water.

GOAT ISLAND

Built in 1859, replacing the original light of 1822, this lighthouse is near the entrance to Cape Porpoise Harbor.

To photograph this lighthouse take Hwy 9 from US 1 to Wharf St. to the fishing pier. You will be able to view the lighthouse and take photographs from the pier.

CAPE NEDDICK/NUBBLE ISLAND

This light is one of the most photographed and visited in Maine. It was first illuminated on July 1, 1879 and extensive renovations were completed in 1990. From this picturesque spot on a clear day you will also be able to see Boon Island Lighthouse, standing tall six and a half miles out from the point. Cape Neddick Light is located on Nubble Island which was first named Savage Rock in 1602.

On November 30, 1842 the vessel the **Isidore** crashed to pieces at Bald Head Cliffs just north of Cape Neddick. The **Isidore** has become the lengendary phantom ship of the Maine coast sailing the high seas with her phantom crew.

The popularity of Cape Neddick Lightstation with photographers, artists, and lighthouse enthusiasts was proven when the Coast Guard painted the red brick oil house white. So many people called and wrote to protest the changing of the color that the oil house was repainted to its original bright red. Upon close examination you will see that the tops of posts on the railing surrounding the lantern room are shaped like miniature lighthouses.

The rocks at Sohier Park are fun to climb on to enjoy the magnitude of the ocean or just sun yourself, and you will always see a lot of people here. While here, be sure to visit Lighthouse Restaurant on Nubble Road. From their dining room you will be able to enjoy the spectacular, panoramic view of Nubble Light.

To reach Sohier Park and view the lighthouse, take US 1 in York to US 1A to York Beach area to Nubble Road and then to Sohier Park Road. Also while in the area, stay to tour York Harbor, the walking tour is well worth the time.

BOON ISLAND

Boon Island Light is located 6 1/2 miles southeast of Cape Neddick on a rocky barren island that is only 700 feet long and less than a third of a mile wide. Can you image living on this isolated rock as did keeper William Willams for 27 long years?

It would take an entire book to detail all the stories and tales behind the history of Boon Island. as well as to verify the many conflicting dates of events.

In 1710, the Nottingham Galley was shipwrecked here and the crew was stranded on Boon Island and reportedly resorted to cannibalism before being rescued.

In the period of 1710 to 1790 there were many shipwrecks around Boon Island resulting in the first tower being erected in July 1780, however the beacon was not installed until 1800. This tower was 50 feet high, 16 feet in diameter with an octagonal base. A violent storm on October 9, 1805 destroyed and washed away this tower. In the summer of 1805, a temporary stone tower with a beacon at the top was erected and in 1811 another lighthouse was built only to be destroyed in 1831. Another violent storm resulted in the building of yet another lighthouse. The current lighthouse, built in 1852, is the **tallest** in Maine at 137 feet high and is 25 feet in diameter at the base and 12 feet in diameter at the top.

Keepers who manned this barren lightstation at one time, communicated to the mainland by the use of carrier pigeons. After 167 years of being a manned station Boon Island Light became automated in 1978.

The black and white photograph is courtesy of the United States Coast Guard.

Boon Island Light as it appears today

FORT McCLARY STATE PARK
&
FORT FOSTER PARK
Kittery, Maine

Originally referred to as Pepperell's Garrison in 1690 after William Pepperell, a prominent Kittery citizen, it became Fort McClary during the Revolution. The old blockhouse, pictured on this page, was built in 1812 and is the most visible point of the old fort. All the forts in and around Portsmouth Harbor were so heavily fortified, they prevented a British attack during the War of 1812. At the outbreak of the Civil War, extensive modifications were started. The work was then abandoned when the North realized there was no threat to Portsmouth Harbor from the Confederacy or its possible foreign allies. The large granite slabs can be seen just as they were left when modifications were abruptly stopped.

To reach Fort McCary State Park take US 1, in Kittery, to Rt. 103, which will lead directly to the fort. There are picnic facilities and ample parking is available here. While here, you will be able to obtain great views and photographs of **Portsmouth Harbor Lighthouse**, Fort Constitution, as well as the old Portsmouth Naval prison across the harbor. You will also be able to view Whaleback Lighthouse and Jerry's Point Lifesaving Station from here; however, for better views proceed down Rt 103 to Chauncey Creek Road and turn right onto Pocahontas Road, go over the bridge and turn right to Fort Foster Park.

Fort Foster was built in 1872 and remained an active military installation until 1949. It is now maintained as a park by the town of Kittery, and is accessible year round. The ruins of Fort Foster are impressive and well worth your time. Ample parking and picnic facilities are available. From here you will be able to get the best close up views of **Whaleback Light, Jerry's Point Lifesaving Station**, as well as **Isles of Shoals Light** in the distance.

Blockhouse at Fort McClary, first fort constructed in Maine

NEW HAMPSHIRE

New Hampshire was the first of the 13 colonies to declare its independence from Great Britain

Became a state June 21, 1788 becoming the ninth state

Known as the GRANITE STATE because of its granite industry which at one time ranked top in the nation

33 State Parks

9304 square miles

1300 lakes and ponds

Famous Lake Winnipesaukee has 72 miles of shoreline and 200 islands

Lake Sunapee is one of a few land locked lakes to have lighrthouses

State tree is the White Birch

1058 square miles of the beautiful White Mountain National Forest are located in New Hampshire

Highest mountain in the northeast United States is Mount Washington at 6288 feet

Highest wind velocity ever recorded in the United States was at the summit of Mount Washington, where winds often exceed 200 mph

Oldest summer resort in America is Wolfeboro, New Hampshire

Completed in 1869 the Cog Railway was the first mountain climbing railroad in the world, ascending to the summit of Mount Washington

Top industries are tourism and manufacturing

State motto is LIVE FREE OR DIE

Famous natural landmark is "The Old Main Of the Mountain

International Treaty held in Portsmouth in 1905 ending the Japanese-Russian War

NEW HAMPSHIRE NOTABLES

<u>Franklin Pierce</u>

1804-1869

U.S. House of Representatives 1834-1837

U.S. Senator 1837-1842

Nominated on the 49th ballot for president Became 14th President of the U.S. on March 4, 1853

Lost the nomination for a second term

Served as a Brigadeer General in Mexican-American War

<u>Horace Greeley</u>

1811-1872

Journalist and political leader

Made famous the statement "Go West Young Man, Go West"

<u>Daniel Webster</u>

1782-1852

Orator, lawyer, statesman

U.S. House of Representatives 1823-1827

Secretary of State under Presidents William Harrison and John Tyler

Known for his statement: "Liberty and union now and forever, one and inseperable"

<u>John Stark</u>

1729-1822

Soldier & statesman

Colonel of New Hampshire Minutemen at Battle of Bunker Hill

Author of State Motto "Live Free or Die"

<u>William Plummer</u>

1759-1850

Politian and statesman

U.S. Senator 1802-1807

Governor 1812-1819

In 1820 he cast the only electoral vote against James Monroe for the President of the United States

<u>Amos Tuck</u>

1810-1879

Politian and statesman

One of the original founders of the Republican Party

PORTSMOUTH HARBOR/NEWCASTLE

Referrred to by some as Fort Point Light or Fort Constitution Light, the first lighthouse here in 1771 consisted of a lamp hoisted up a flag pole. It became a wooden tower in 1784 with Captain Titus Salter its first keeper. In 1877, a cast iron tower was constructed 1,000 feet away from the original location and this tower still stands today.

This area was originally named Ft. William and Mary a British stronghold that guarded Portsmouth Harbor. On December 13, 1774, Paul Revere made his first and less famous ride from Boston to Portsmouth to warn the colonists that the British were coming to reinforce Ft. William and Mary. This resulted in the first overt act of the Revolutionary War, when the colonists overpowered the British garrison and made off with military supplies. At the conclusion of the Revolutionary War, the fort was renamed Ft. Constitution.

Also at this location you will be able to see Walbach Tower, one of several fortifications built along the Atlantic Coastline during the War of 1812. These towers were built by General John de Barth Walbach who became second in command of all New England Seacoast defenses. General Walbach at the age of 93, was the oldest General in the history of the United States Army.

The lighthouse refurbished in 1977, can be reached by taking US 1 in Portsmouth to Rt 1B and then to Wentworth Ave by following the signs toward New Castle and Fort Constitution.

The lighthouse is on an active Coast Guard Station which is off-limits to the public, however you can obtain great views and photographs from the walls of the old fort or nearby public parks.

From this location you will be able to view and photograph Whaleback Light and Jerry's Point Lifesaving Station.

Also in the New Castle area, you will want to visit Fort Stark, which overlooks Portsmouth Harbor with spectacular ocean views. Fort Stark served as a military fortification from the Revolutionary War through the Second World War.

WHALEBACK

Whaleback Light, located in the northeast side of Portsmouth Harbor, is actually in Maine waters; however, it was built to guard the entrance to Portsmouth Harbor. The first light was built here in 1820. When the current tower was erected next to it in 1872, the old tower remained standing for several years before it was torn down. The base of the old tower was used to support a red, cylindrical fog signal. The fog signal is now gone, but the base of the original 1820 tower is still there.

The granite tower, which is 59 feet high, and measures 42 feet in diameter, is best photographed from Fort Foster in Kittery, Maine. It can also be photographed from Fort McClary in Kittery, and also from Portsmouth Harbor Light in New Hampshire.

JERRY'S POINT LIFESAVING STATION

This abandoned lifesaving station, one of the last of its kind, is located in Portsmouth Harbor and can be best seen from Fort Foster in Kittery, Maine.

Although many lighthouse preservation groups are doing their utmost to preserve lighthouses, they seem to have forgotten the historically significant, lifesaving stations.

ISLES OF SHOALS

The first Isles of Shoals lighthouse was erected on White Island in 1821. Thomas Leighton built a large hotel on Star Island during his stay as keeper from 1839 to 1847. Leighton's daughter Celia Thaxter became quickly reknowned as the author of many lighthouse poems.

During the early 1700's, Blackbeard the Pirate was chased off Star Island so suddenly that he left one of his many wives behind. She is said to still haunt the island today, waiting for her Pirate husband to return. On a cold, windy night, if you listen to the wind, you may hear her wail, "He shall return." Captain Kidd was also active in this area, and people still search today for the treasures the pirates buried along the New England Coast and its many off shore islands.

Two modern day mysterious shipwrecks occurred near Isles of Shoals, when in 1939, the submarine **Squalus** sank here, and then in 1963, the submarine **Thresher** went to the bottom.

The light can only be photographed by air or boat.

LAKE SUNAPEE

During the Golden Age of Steamboating, which began in 1876, steamboats carried hundreds of passengers from the railroad depots to the Lakeside Landing on Lake Sunapee. From there the tourists took stagecoaches to the New London resort hotels and boarding houses.

In 1891, the 98 foot wooden steamboat *Edmond Burke* was severely damaged when it hit a rocky reef. Due to this wreck, the steamboat owners petitioned the state of New Hampshire to have a lighthouse built on Lake Sunapee. The first lighthouse was built on Loon Island in 1893 at a cost of less than $400. The exact dates are not available; however, it is believed that by 1896 the two additional lighthouses were constructed on Lake Sunapee.

Burkehaven Lighthouse was destroyed by ice in 1936 and rebuilt the same year. In approximately 1896, it was reported that the fire department went to repair Loon Island Lighthouse. During their repairs, the lighthouse caught fire, and with only one bucket available, they were able to extinquish the fire with lake water and completed their repairs. In 1960, lightning struck Loon Island Lighthouse causing it to burn to the ground. It was rebuilt that same year.

Today, the New Hampshire Department of Marine Control maintains these three lighthouses from May through October.

In the summer months, the **M/V Mt. Sunapee II** offers tours of Lake Sunapee and viewing of all three lighthouses. For exact times and fees you may contact Captain David Hargbol, P.O. Box 345, Sunapee Harbor, New Hampshire 03782, (603)763-4030.

Loon Island Lighthouse with Mount Kearsarge in the background. Loon Island and Herrick Cove photographs courtesy of Captain David Hargbol.

Burkehaven Lighthouse

Herrick Cove Lighthouse

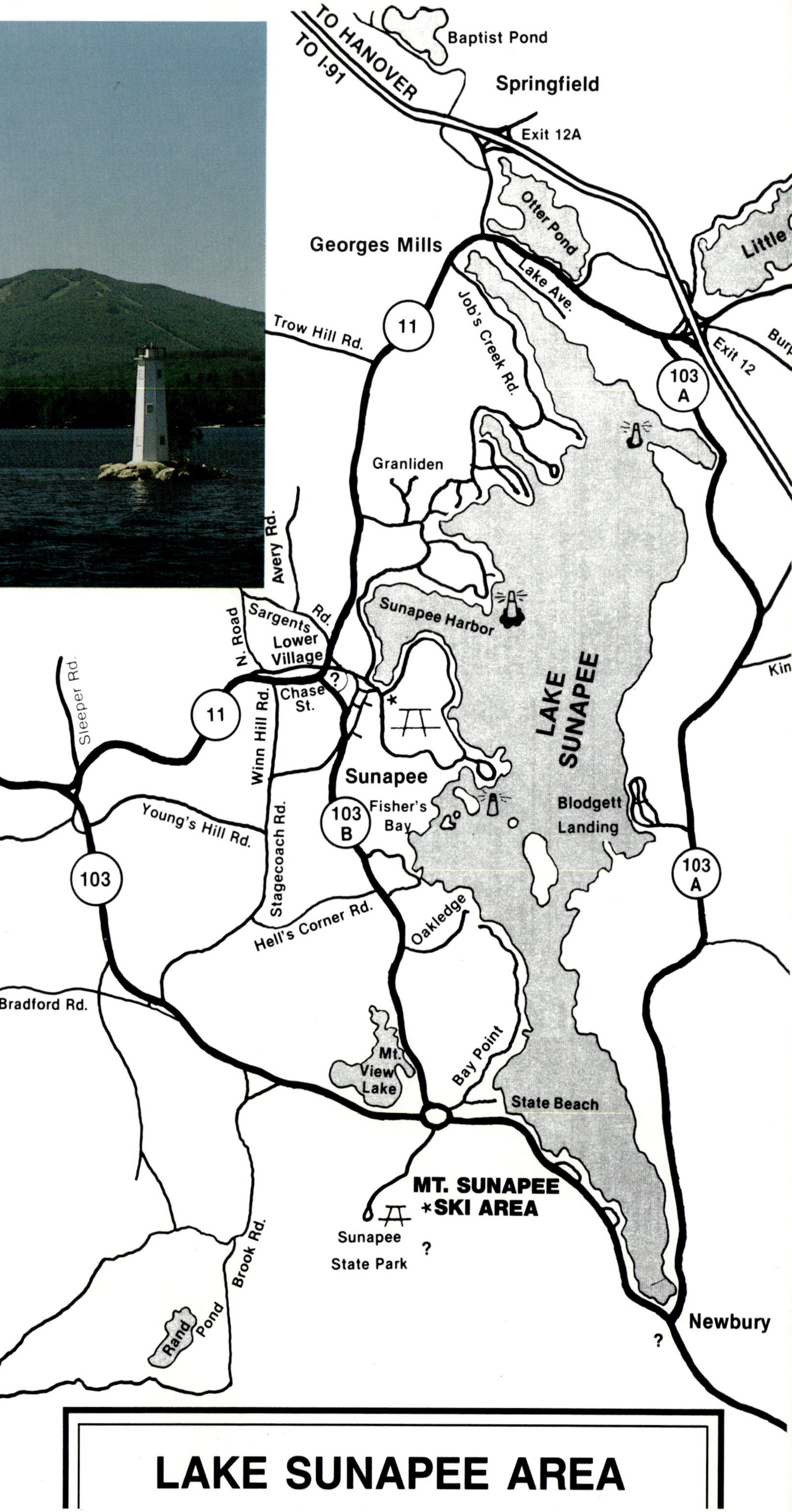

LAKE SUNAPEE AREA

THE FAMILY LIGHTHOUSE

The Family Lighthouse is a dream come true for Nancy and Irving Silverman. The fell in love with lighhouses when they first came to Maine 25 years ago. Their interest became a passion and they began collecting lighthouse memorabilia, oral history of retired lighthouse keepers, and everything published about lighthouses. They decided to build their own private lighthouse above their Nancy Neale antique Typecraft shop to combine their dual interest in Maine. The Harding Wharf with its historic 65 lobster bouy wall is one of the most photographed sights on the Maine coastline. The Family Lighthouse on the Harding Wharf was dedicated in October of 1990.

To view the lighthouse, from Ellsworth take Rt 3 south to Mount Desert Island, to Rt 102, toward Tremont, watch for the small sign that says Bernard, Steamboat Wharf and follow the road. It can also be viewed from across the water in the town of Bass Harbor.

Mr. Silverman is researching private lighthouses in the United States. If you know of any private lighthouses, he would appreciate hearing from you by writing to him at: IRVING SILVERMAN, STEAMBOAT WHARF, BERNARD, MAINE 04612.

The sketch at left was furnished courtesy of Nancy and Irving Silverman.

LIGHTHOUSE REPLICAS

The Lighthouse is used by hundreds of businesses and communities as a symbol of strength, safety, and security.

LIGHTHOUSE REALTY - BUILT 1932
ROUTE 302, NAPLES MAINE (207) 693-6464

SHIPS QUARTERDECK RESTAURANT, US 1,
KITTERY, MAINE (207) 439-5198

WELCOME TO SOUTH PORTLAND, MAINE

PUBLIC PARKING LOT, YORK, MAINE

LIGHTHOUSE CONDOMINIUMS, ROUTE 1, WELLS, MAINE

OLD ORCHARD BEACH, MAINE

LIGHTHOUSE RESTAURANT MAIN STREET P.O. BOX 223, SEAL HARBOR, MAINE (207)276-3958. OPEN MAY TO NOVEMBER.

THE LIGHTHOUSE LIGHTING CENTER, US 1, KENNEBUNKPORT, MAINE

LIGHTHOUSE GALLERY OF GIFTS

Located on Rt 1 in Searsport, Maine, this lighthouse replica was built in 1988. It is open to the public during store hours, May 1 through December 24.

There is a lovely view of Penobscot Bay from the lantern room.

SCHOONER MINI GOLF COURSE.

Rt 5, south of Rt 195, toward Old Orchard Beach, Maine.

ROCKLAND AREA CHAMBER OF COMMERCE AND INFORMATION CENTER

MODEL OF PEMAQUID LIGHTHOUSE ON DISPLAY AT SHORE VILLAGE MUSEUM

THE UNITED STATES LIGHTHOUSE SOCIETY

PRESERVING AMERICA'S LIGHTHOUSES
through Education and Research

The U.S. Lighthouse Society is a national non-profit historical and educational organization dedicated to restoration and preservation of lighthouses lightships, and lighthouse lore. The society maintains a research library and photo archives, organizes regional tours, takes on related preservation projects (using volunteer members) and publishes a quarterly Bulletin. If interested call: (415) 362-7255

or write:

THE UNITED STATES
LIGHTHOUSE SOCIETY
244 Kearny St., 5th Floor
San Francisco, CA 94108

WELCOME ABOARD! The Society's goal is to strongly support the preservation of these important symbols of our maritime heritage. If interested in joining, ($25 per year), telephone 415/362-7255.

"Classic American Lighthouses"

All East Coast lighthouses are featured in this limited-edition, FULL-COLOR offset lithograph print. Printed on 100% rag paper, the print includes a Certificate of Authenticity, your receipt, and a flyer with other lighthouse prints now available. ("Classic American Lighthouses II" due out late in 1991)

Print sheet 7-1/2" x 20" $34.00 + $4 pkg.
Shipped flat within 5 days via UPS

Make checks payable to:

Mrs. Bev. Schreiber
5831 106th St. S.W.
Everett, WA 98204

VISA & MC accepted
1-206-742-3131

Lighthouse Sweatshirt

Lighthouses of the Northeast, *Style #576*
Cotton blend printed front and back.
Navy on white or grey. M, L, XL $32;
XXL $35; S&H $3 ea.; VISA,
Discover, MC, check or MO. Toll free
1-800-873-0569 or write:

Ruby's Designs
3950 E. Milham Rd.
Kalamazoo, MI 49001

Michigan residents add 4% sales tax. Allow 3 to 6 weeks delivery.

ADVERTISEMENT FOR CARTER BROTHERS DEPICTING MOVADO WATCHES ON PORTLAND HEAD LIGHT.

PHOTO COURTESY OF CARTER BROTHERS COMPANY, PORTLAND, MAINE, FINE JEWELERS SINCE 1854.

There are many tour boats and charter services operating off the coast of Maine, so many in fact, that it would be impossible to list them all. The following is a partial list of some of the tour boats that you can take to obtain great photos of lighthouses.

Since schedules, fees, and the months of operation change throughout the year, you should always call or write to them for exact information.

This list does not constitute an endorsement, it is simply furnished as general information.

ISLANDER & LINEKIN II

Pier 6

Boothbay, Harbor, Maine 04538

(207)633-2500

ARGO TOUR BOAT

Boothbay Harbor, Maine 04538

(207)633-4925 or 633-5090

BOOTHBAY STEAMSHIP CO

at Tug Boat Inn

Boothbay Harbor, Maine 04538

(207)633-BOAT or 633-2628

CAP'N FISH'S SIGHTSEEING BOAT

Pier 1

Boothbay Harbor, Maine 04538

(207)633-3244 or 633-2626

"BREAKAWAY" CRUISES

Capt. Pete Ripley

Box 860

East Boothbay Harbor, Maine 04544

BALMY DAYS

Box 102

Boothbay Harbor, Maine 04538

(207)633-2284

HARDY II

at Maine Maritime Museum

Bath, Maine

(207)443-1316

FRENCHMANS BAY BOATING CO.

1 West Street

Bar Harbor, Maine 04609

(207)288-5741

ARCADIAN & FRENCHMAN BAY

Bar Harbor, Maine 04609

(207)288-3571 or 288-3322

BAY & SUNSET CRUISES AND ARCADIAN WHALE WATCHER

Golden Anchor Pier

Bar Harbor, Maine 04609

(207)288-9794 or 288-9726

HARDY III

Shaws Fish & Lobster Wharf Rest.

New Harbor, Maine 04554

(207)677-2026 or 882-7909

PALAWA

P.O. Box 9715

Portland, Maine 04104

(207)773-2163

BAY VIEW CRUISES "LADY JOAN"

Fishermans Wharf

Commercial Street

Portland, Maine

(207)774-3578

LONGFELLOW CRUISE LINE

One Long Wharf

Portland, Maine 04101

(207)774-3578

THE BITTER END

P.O. Box 1230

Rockland, Maine 04841

(207)594-9040

THE FRIENDSHIP SLOOP "GRACE O'MALLEY"

Rockland Public Landing

Rockland, Maine

(207)594-0661

PENOBSCOT BAY CRUISES

Camden Public Landing

Camden, Maine 04843

CASCO BAY LINES

P.O. Box 4656

Portland, maine 04112

(207)744-7871

Our special thanks and appreciation are extended to the following:

KEN BLACK and BOB DAVIS

Shore Village Museum

104 Limerock Street

Rockland, Maine 04841

C. F. KINGLER

Commander, U.S. Coast Guard

Chief, Signal Managment Branch

Washington, D.C. 20593

THE NATIONAL ARCHIVES

Still Pictures Branch

Washington, D.C. 20408

We would also like to thank the following pilots and air charter services, and would highly recommend their services to photograph lighthouses by air.

IAN LEISHMAN

Maine Aviation Corporation

1127 Westbrook St.

Portland, Maine 04102

(207)775-5635

CECIL JACOBSON

Downeast Flying Service

P.O. Box 252

Wiscasset, Maine 04578

(800)752-6378

MICHAEL BALL

Penobscot Air Service

Owls Head Airport

Rockland, Maine 04841

(207)596-6211

If you have a wish to become involved in lighthouse preservation or simply to be informed, we would suggest joining one or all of the following organizations. All of them publish newsletters and membership fees are nominal.

UNITED STATES LIGHTHOUSE SOCIETY

244 Kearney Street, 5th Floor

San Francisco, California 94108

(415)362-7255

SHORE VILLAGE MUSEUM & HISTORICAL SOCIETY

104 Limerock Street

Rockland, Maine 04841

(207)594-0311

LIGHTSHIP NANTUCKET, INC.

58 Fore Street

Portland, Maine 04101

(207)775-1181

THE LIGHTHOUSE PRESERVATION SOCIETY

P.O. Box 736

Rockport, Massachusetts 01966

(508)281-6336

GREAT LAKES LIGHTHOUSE SOCIETY

P.O. Box 580

Allen Park, Michigan 48101

THE AMERICAN LIGHTHOUSE HISTORICAL SOCIETY

P.O. Box 50186

Jacksonville Beach, Florida 32250

(904)241-8845

If you wish to research information on lighthouses, we would encourage you to visit:

MAINE HISTORICAL PRESERVATION COMMISSION
55 Capitol Street
Augusta, Maine
(207)289-2033

MAINE HISTORICAL SOCIETY
485 Congress Street
Portland, Maine
(207)774-1822